Bringing The Black Boy To Manhood: The Passage

Nathan Hare, PH. D & Julia Hare, Ed. D

T0165665

African American IMAGES

I have known Nathan and Julia Hare over 30 years. We presented numerous times together. I wanted to keep their scholarship alive. I thank Nathan for giving me permission. Sincerely, Dr. Jawanza Kunjufu February 1, 2021.

CONTENTS

BRINGING
THE BLACK BOY TO MANHOOD:
THE PASSAGE

THE COMMITMENT

A syndicated columnist tells how a Howard University professor, a friend of his, called up one night in a dither about an encounter with three boisterous black teenagers. The teenagers, "loud, unrestrained and shockingly obscene," had barged into a lunchtime soul food restaurant in the Nation's Capitol. It wasn't that the professor's own generation hadn't used some of the same language as the boys. But there was a difference: "we never would have said such things in the presence of adults."[1]

The professor further confessed a nagging fear of the

boys. "These kids are going to be lost unless we figure out some way of rescuing them. But what?" The columist echoed him. "We black middle class individuals who wish to help the underclass are helpless, idea-less witnesses to a near total breakdown. Can anything be done?"

The *New York Times*[2] carries the story of two black boys, Jonah and Edmund Perry, from a broken Harlem home. Jonah and Edmund had come under the influence of A Better Chance, or ABC, program and graduated from such prep schools as Phillips Exeter Academy and Hartford's Westminster School. Now 19, Jonah was looking forward to his sophomore year at Cornell. Edmund, having studied abroad for a year in Spain, had gained admission to Yale, the University of California at Berkeley, Stanford *and* the University of Pennsylvania.

But now Edmund was dead, at 17, and Jonah was being indicted and charged with assault and attempted robbery of a highly regarded plainclothes policeman. The charges had grown out of an altercation in which the officer shot Phillip dead one night in June in the quiet shadows of Columbia University.

Examples are legion. In a cover roundup on immigrants, *Time* magazine admits that African-Americans came here in chains (as forced immigrants) and only in the past 20 years were fully enfranchised even by law. The magazine now sees "two black Americas"--a "growing black middle class" and "an entrenched underclass stuck at the very bottom of society...who appear less capable of economic survival than the tenacious new immigrants" they increasingly resent and envy.

While the new immigrants quickly rise, "three centuries after the first slave ship arrived [with black Americans], "a pattern repeats itself." The pattern: when other immigrants move up as small businessmen and then depart black neighborhoods, blacks are left "unable to capitalize on the opportunities, leaving many of the stores abandoned and boarded up."

Though readily conceding the full force of racism, which compels black Americans, among the oldest Americans, to confront "the land of opportunity denied," the writer concludes that the problem may have something to do with the attitude of the vast underclass of blacks and the circumstance of "a large percentage of them from fragmented families and households headed by women."

There will be gnashing of teeth--and some of it un-doubtedly necessary--by black leaders and intellectuals in the months and years ahead. There will be bouncing of outraged eyeballs and splitting of hairs to protect and defend the black image and perhaps to devise programs and funding proposals to solve the problem of black immobility and racist intran-sigence. There will be "crisis" conferences, summits, rallies, seminars, marches, parades and floats. But what will they profit us if the problem remains?

The black race is like an unsteady palace, gigantic and ornate, teetering at its base while people gather around with cranes and complex machinery. The people squeal and squeech and prop the palace up, feverishly, pompously, work-ing to repair it at its cracks and wobbly ceiling, when all the while the problem of the building's unsteadiness is a few miss-ing bricks and broken mortar from its now all but invisible foundation.

When we first began to ponder the issue of black

of excellence in education among blacks to the level of excellence in athletics and music. After Speaker Brown had lowered his gavel, the West Coast Regional Director of the NAACP, leaned over and whispered: "I like that. How could that be done?" The momentary response whispered back was: "I don't know. I can imagine an academic Olympics for high school and junior high school children, where trophies would be given..."

Some months later, we heard the Chairman of the Board of the National Association for the Advancement of Colored People, Margaret Bush Wilson, being interviewed on a radio talk show discussing a new NAACP program.[4]

Her words were essentially what we had said at the education conference in 1975. Since that time, ACT-SO, evolved as one of the NAACP's most successful projects. We are inspired by the NAACP's accomplishments with our idea. We now propose to insert another, more fundamental, brick into the battered foundation of black socialization in America.

The Question

In a time when social failure is concomitant to the confusion and uncertainty of a problem-laden world, when children no longer respect their parents or find peace with themselves and the uneasy society that will soon be theirs, who is to blame? Is it enough, where families daily crumble, where parenting is diminished and even discouraged, where child abuse is rampant and, if anything inflamed anew by conventional efforts to rectify it, where disrespect and conflict rage as the acquiescent norm in human relations, where workshops to aid "communication" between men and women in love cannot stem the tide or heal the romantic-sexual rift, is it enough to blame the age-old waywardness and reluctance of children and youth?

Can parents merely point their fingers at the teachers? Can teachers, in all sincerity and truth, blame the parents? Can they both blame the preacher? The courts? The politicians? The policemen? The social workers? The probation officers? The counselors? The therapists? The social scientists? Can they blame the intellectuals, the experts, or the ignorant? Can we merely critique the lower classes we daily convict in spite of our mushrooming and costly "services" to correct them? Can they in turn blame only us?

Clearly, our problem (and therefore its solution) is centered in a range of heartrending, festering, questions. For instance, why do black boys rebel against their parent's teachings and their wishes? Why do so many parents now turn their backs on them? Why are so many of our children turning away to suicide and dope, delinquency and crime? Why are so many giving up on the hopes and the dreams of our ancestors, our pride and our traditions?

Why, increasingly, can't we any longer rear our children in the way that we once knew? Why is homicide so overwhelmingly a problem between young black men in their twenties? Why is rape so disproportionately visited upon black women by black men? Why are there more young black men, intelligent and potentially productive black men, vibrant and virile, in prison? Why more in prison than in college? Why do our scholars complain so passionately against the high flunkout rate of black athletes, when the attrition rate is similarly high among black college students who don't play any ball? Why do so many children drop out of school, then in turn out of acceptable society?

Why, in the era of the pill and the chemical-surgical arsenal of family planning agencies, is teenage pregnancy a growing national scandal? Why are children just as likely to be left with only one parent as not to? Why must so many black women complain that the boys they seek to raise, let alone the ones they and their daughters will love and marry, can't seem to grow up to be real men?

Treatises and proposals galore have been and will be written on the answers to these and related questions. But increasingly they no longer will satisfy. Even if we could ferret out and agree upon the questions, let alone the answers, their very magnitude and multiplicity might simply overwhelm us.

Now, we have no wish to deny -- and readily concede -- the large number of adjusted, productive and inimitable black individuals today. They are not at issue here. We also have recorded the growing number of white beggars and degenerates on the streets. Nor do we have any wish to release a recalcitrant white society from its relentless disregard of our humanity.

The superiority, even dominance, of our race in a wide range of fields from which we previously were excluded, the acknowledged efficiency and strength of many black women, black excellence, our worldwide popularity and influence in music and accessible entertainment, our accomplishments as guarded tokens in a diversity of fields, are clearly apparent. Our very survival in the vicious grip of racist denial, all testify to our basic and inherent capacities as a people. What would appear to have been broken is not our resolve or our spirit but the control and capability in the *socialization* of our children.

We are steadily losing the ability -- indeed the authority increasingly undermined or usurped by state (government) and commercial institutions -- to rear our children.[5] We can't ensure that they will become what we wish for them to be, or they wish for themselves, nor even that they will become and behave as socially acceptable, let alone successful or happy, adults. We are less and less able to give them the motivation (provide them a motive) for living up to our ideals and aspirations.

If we can't remove the enemy we have internalized and so pervasively hold within, can we really expect the enemy from without to reverse himself? If there are black people who in spite of racial restrictions nevertheless prevail on a higher plane, is it possible to provide for all or many blacks the protection against social invective which they enjoy? What is their secret? Is it anything more than comformity and assimilation to the master's will? Can we willingly transmit (for our own designs) the tenacity, incentive and clarity of purpose without losing pride in race, or consciousness as a people?

The Call

Must we wait until we have all the answers? Must we continue to do "empirical" research in the quest for technical knowledge that fails to apply while our problem grows stronger with each passing day? Our knowledge is already great and growing along with our demise. We have more and more knowledge and less and less understanding while we continue to fail our acknowledged potential. We must find something we can do to correct the things we may never fully understand. We must begin to cut through the complexity of our existence with a few, *so many as one,* basic solution.

Proceeding with caution (for the task before us is both elementary and complex, as complicated and perilous as the process of unraveling and untangling a twisted cord in order to get to its essential straightness), let us begin with the problem of personal mastery.

Personal Mastery & the Locus of Control

One of the most crucial dilemmas -- and one that can cripple the confidence and motivation of the black individual (whose self image is gained in part through the "looking glass" of white society) is the anchorage of the *locus of control.*

As psychologists conceive it, how one behaves in the struggle to mobilize one's resources for self-fulfillment is dictated by whether one sees the center of the control of one's destiny situated in oneself (internal) or amid the snares and snarls of fate and fortune (external). Who is responsible for your life and future?

The individualistic orientation of our society demands that we think of the *locus of control* as mainly internal ("everybody's reponsible for his own soul's salvation", and "God helps those who help themselves"). By contrast, black psychologists[6] have understandably sought to call attention to the other side of the coin, the external, how differences in our fates and fortunes affect us as blacks particularly, unjustly, in a racist society. But, when all is said and done, we all know that life is actually a complex intermixture of both the internal *and* the external. What trips up the black individual too readily is the tendency to confuse the question of who is responsible with who is to blame.

On the one hand, we ought not to close our eyes to the restraints and restrictions of racism that are real. On the other hand, we must avoid the psychological trap of expecting the same forces we say are oppressing us to turn around and lift us up or even to show us the way. A young black man comes into therapy from the hospital. He is a genius by IQ tests. The physician has told him, he reports, that if he keeps on drinking and returns to the hospital again for his pancreatitis, the physician won't be able to save him.

In therapy, when the conversation turns to his current academic performance, he reveals that, despite his gifted academic background, he presently isn't doing very well. As justification, he explains that "he needs a drink to put up with them white folks," forgetting that he is killing himself wth alcohol.

You cannot depend on the selfsame forces that keep you down to lift you up. In fact, when you give up or fail to grapple with that oppression according to your best capabilities, even if you allow that oppression to get you down, to defeat you, in part you are collaborating with your oppressor. You owe it to the cause of black uplift and freedom, if not to yourself, to survive and perhaps in your own way to thrive as a part of your personal mission.

In the days before integration took on a cover of assimilation, black parents customarily and intuitively, routinely, sought to prepare the black child's perspective on the locus of control. "A black person has to be twice as good to get a chance. So you have to work, try, twice as hard." "Don't you stop now, don't you set down on the stairs because times are getting kinder hard."

These days black parents are more inclined, if any thing, to seek to protect their children from any acute thing, to seek to protect their children from any acute awareness of the harsh realities of racist oppression, reflecting perhaps the polyanna psychology on which black intellectuals operate in our time when they typically equate an account of the consequences of racism as "blaming the victim." Having so defined it, they are able to deny and ignore that victimization, that oppression which leaves no mark on the psyche. We must return to some of the old ways that worked, taking the best and leaving the rest alone. Those simple techniques which we have lost may prove far more effective in time than denial and thoughtless imitation of the models of our oppression.

Why the Male

In every human society yet known, of any enduring significance, there are of course two genders - male and female. All societies for which there is sufficient record have been patriarchal. Though many have been *matrilineal*, tracing the ancestry through the mother's line, and women have stood and often stand out as individual rulers or queens, a variety of office holders, there is no anthropological evidence for a society where women as a group ruled men as a group, i.e., *matriarchal*.

Throughout the animal kingdom, in fact, the male has appeared to be needed mainly to help protect the female during the reproduction and rearing of the offspring.[8] Thus, in human societies, elaborate systems have arisen to regulate the male's function. Consequently in a patriarchal society where men predominate among the rulers, it is the oppressed male that poses the primary threat to the male rulers, and it is the oppressed male that must be derailed.

If the male of the group is weakened or eliminated, this automatically impacts upon the women and children, the family, and the social stability of the group or race. There can be no viable race without a viable patriarch in a patriarchal society. In the patriarchal world of the past and the foreseeable future, it is the male and his performance that constitute the missing link to family stability and racial survival.

Most statistics today confirm the popular awareness of an acute black male decimation, from homicide, crime, mental illness, addiction and just about every source imaginable, consequent *and* leading to socio-economic insufficiency. The black male is hampered in his performance of his role and accordingly loses and misses a certain sense of purpose, function, personal importance, of family and group commitment.

Although this does not include all black males, it includes far too many. In any case, the male is the one that people say is not performing up to par in the black race. The black male gives everybody pause; he is the one that must play a more salient part, it is thoroughly believed, in holding the black family together. He is the one complained about by women, and sometimes men, and the one most decimated by current social institutions.[9] Despite a concession to black female suffering and abuse, we as a group are not crying about the black woman's crippled initiative and depletion. In fact, black women feel -- and men echo them -- that they're doing a pretty good job, that it is black men as a group who must do much better.

We admit these problems but increasingly join forces with those who would further neglect and deride black male development. The socialization of black boys in today's fractured family life is left too often to the peer groups and the streets. Street education is often maladaptive, even antithetical, oppositional, to school performance and parental teaching.

There is some evidence of the probability that playing the dozens and related rapping on the part of ghetto black boys is a *re-creation*, albeit in the pathological form, of the pre-European African ritual function of trickstering.[10] An African consultant points out that trickstering in Africa -- in Nigeria, for instance -- typically had the boy putting down the father in this verbal game of one-up-manship to manhood. In the absence of adult design and ritual supervision -- and perhaps reflecting the matrifocal character of a decimated male supply and male functioning in Afro-America -- the boy puts down the *mother* instead. When adults neglect or fail to rear the children, the children fall back on the quixotic guidance of the peer group. The peer group sets the standards and the perimeters of their behavior. It builds disdain and contempt for the values and advice of the parents. In the absence of the father and his relentless model for the boy, with no one of authority and forcefulness to backup the mother's decrees, the boy is all the more easily instigated to oppose his mother's authority. In the best of such circumstances, half of the parental force is missing.

Unlike the girl whose first love object is of the same sex,

the boy must gain a certain separateness in his identity formation. For bio-cultural reasons, the boy becomes sensitive in latency to the male/female dichotomy. He typically endeavors to pull away from the mother's control, indeed the feminine world of baby sitters, elementary school teachers, and, in a way, girls. A fired-up interest in manly sports combine with his disdain and sometimes disgust with his feminine possibilities to comprise the "masculine protest" in which he seeks to confirm his masculine identity, his differentness from the female, including perhaps a reluctance to be kissed, especially in public view by his mother. All in all, the project of masculine protest can become something of a feat.

For females toward the end of latency, there is typically the crisis of menstruation and its physical sequelae to signal the indelible fact of womanhood and the woman's biosocial imperatives. For the male there is no corresponding *biological jolt*. His awareness of his puberty and his potentialities are more subtle and bound to the dictates of sexual pleasure as over against the sobering qualities of the female's concomitant pain and pregnability. Hence, societies historically have struggled through initiation rites and related feats, ordeals, scarification, and artificial traumas, to provide the boy with a *psychosocial jolt* into manhood.

Many parents have now come to maturity under post-industrial society's new norms of permissiveness and parental commitment or preoccupation outside the home. They've grown up essentially unparented themselves. In a deeper sense, they no longer know how to parent. Rather than rely on their memory pictures of how their parents dealt with them, they may depend on how-to books, searching for some unknown formulas or techniques. This very search impresses them with the discouraging possibility that some workable parenting technique exists but continues to elude them. This in turn compounds their feelings of parental inadequacy and guilt and can lead to further ingratiation to the child.

Even if the child does not sense and exploit his advantage, the parent is stymied by the feeling that she/he does not have the right to determine the child's proper behavior. At the same time, parents have in recent times collaborated with the powers-that-be to take authority and discipline away from the teacher in the school. Thus in too many central city ghetto schools, the teacher's endeavor to discipline the children demands priority over the teaching. In some classrooms, consequently, there is neither discipline nor teaching.

Now the teachers have in turn joined forces with the apparatus of the state to take away parental authority. This is being accomplished through a "child abuse" protection movement and other regulations which undermine parental authority and precipitously remove children from the home within the emerging hysteria of helping those who do need help. Authority increasingly is shifted away from the agents of nurturance and development (home and school) to the agents of punishment and rehabilitation (police, courts, social workers, foster homes, counselors, therapists).

In this context, it becomes necessary to find the means to infuse the children with what is lost without discipline in a demanding situation. For the black boy, we must find ways to punctuate his psyche with commitment for family and race, community and nation, with motivation for responsibility, along with personal mastery.[11]

Because we have lost control of our culture and our children's socialization, many black youth suffer an extended adolescence. Boys reach *physical puberty* readily enough; indeed, more precociously than their white counterparts.[12] But it is far more difficult, in an oppressive situation, to gain *social* *puberty*. We must recognize and actualize the difference between physical and social puberty in the black boy's development, just as there's a difference between physical potency and social potency. Indeed, blocked from the avenues to social power and position, social potency, the black boy may too often feel impelled to over-compensate in the physical.

What we need therefore, is some way to bring the black boy to manhood, to highlight and sharpen the focus of the importance and significance of being a man. It must be clear in the outset that there is a difference between being a man and a child, between being a man and a woman. Otherwise, we must not stand perplexed when we discover that more and more men have confused, or failed to develop, the art and feeling of being a man.

We must now be in search of a way to give the black boy a sense of becoming a man, a clearer sense of self and of purpose, responsibility to his roles as father and husband, a sacredness of self and others in the context of a more attentive family and community network of adult endorsement. We must begin to point him in the direction of manly commitment and responsibility. This acknowledges that there is a difference between becoming a physical *sexual* man and becoming a *social* man (a moral and jural condition which extends, or should, far beyond the trappings and execution of uncommitted sexuality).

When we look back to see how we came to our present predicament, going back as far as our African origins, to find out and assess what we lost that was worth saving for our present, we discover that many things of value have been stripped away. One of the things that have been eradicated, with few effective artificial replacements (in contrast to technological development) is the "ritualization of social relationships."[13]

Customs, traditions, rituals and ceremony, for instance, while sometimes punitive and malfunctional and in need of change or repair, are nevertheless as veins and arteries to the body, like the wiring of a radio or an electrical plant. Without the connectives there is a breakdown in continuity of flow, a shortage, somewhere in the system. Although it may generally not be advisable to borrow lost cultural elements entirely intact from the African past, we may neverthless begin to learn from their example and to reconstruct what is necessary and appropriate to the present.

We have neglected and even shunned this process at our peril. At the very time when the male and his role are too often missing from the household, when the child does not have a daily model, sometimes does not know exactly what his father does for a living, sometimes doesn't know his father, when many fathers are not available to their children except at best on a fractionalized basis, the benefits of custom, ceremony, faith and ritual acculturation have been discarded and derided for us as a people.

In pre-colonial Africa, customs, rituals and ceremonies not only regulated the roles of the people; they also gave special qualities and purposes to the land, the "thingira" ("bachelors quarters" in the Gikuyu society of Kenya), animals, and any other objects under given circumstances. These were thereby invested with the sacred and the mysterious as in the church sanctuary of today, where few unholy men would dare to go for antagonistic purposes. Roles too, now multiplying but increasingly despised, could be agreed upon, as in the case of the idea of masculine commitment and responsibility to family, to women and children. Then, through ritual, custom and ceremony, these roles could be invested with the idea of the holy, the sacred, and the imperatives of mystery.

We have tended to lose even the "ceremonial of etiquette" so vital in pre-European Africa, where precisely "the greater the multiplicity of undifferentiated and overlapping roles, the more the ritual to separate them." When we lost these, with little or no replacements, we lost not only coherence of purpose and function but also fundamental connecting linkages among ourselves and our prodigy.

Social scientists of a wide range of ideological and ethnic perspectives have concluded that "there is no evidence that people living in a secular urbanized world have less need of ritualized expression for their transistions from one status to another."[15] Note the lingering importance of graduation ceremonies at schools and colleges, weddings and funerals, and the way that Confirmation and Barmitvahs signal the milestones and status changes in our lives. Rituals reinforce and imprint both duty and propriety.

THE PASSAGE takes account of the principle of psychological imprint. An example of a psychological imprinting is contained in an experiment where it was discovered that ducklings taught that the ethnologist was their mother would continue to think so and to follow him instead of the mother duck.[16] Other studies include the finding that a child mistakenly dressed and treated for the wrong gender cannot, after the age of two, be reversed in his/her gender identity.[17]

In our society today, baptism, for instance, is often an important element in a child's religious validation and sanctity. Graduations of all kinds are ceremonialized and ritualized turning points. Birthdays are celebrated with candles to match the years and consequences for failing to blow them out in one breath.

In THE PASSAGE, we are considering a more total transformation. It is a prelude to a metamorphosis, to manhood. In time, hopefully THE PASSAGE will become as universal and essential as birthdays and graduation ceremonies.

Where do we begin?

It may be instructive for us to follow the black child hypothetically through the Eriksonian stages of psychosocial development which, at least in an embryonic way, reaches beyond Freud's psychosexual stages of personality development, to take account of the impact of society on the individual. Based on Erik Erikson's work launched in his book, *Childhood and Society*,[18] psychoanalysts and other psychologists broke away from a narrow Freudian emphasis on the dominant force of the inner drives. They are learning to acknowledge that, while the internal feelings are crucial enough, they must operate in and are affected by the struggle with the forces from without. This struggle begins with birth (and even in the prenatal womb). Erikson demonstrated in any case that the struggle for identity development was lifelong, or ideally could be. More importantly it was epigenetic, meaning that trauma in one stage, or failure to successfully meet the challenge presented there, invariably handicapped the individual's successful negotiation of the challenges of subsequent stages. It is something like a sprinter getting off to a bad start, or a loaf of baking bread with improper or incomplete ingredients, a castle with a weak or crumbling foundation.

Beginning in infancy, there is the dilemma of *basic trust vs. mistrust*. The infant child must come to feel that the mothering one will be there, will return when she goes away. In the process the child holds on but also learns to let go. *Hope* is the basic strength (or psychosocial crisis) that must be met and developed.

Late in the second year of life, or the period of early childhood, the dominant theme becomes the development of the child's self will, negating the mother's or caretaker's, saying no to the mother in order in time more genuinely to say yes. The challenge is *autonomy vs. shame or self doubt.* Toilet training will become an issue for many at this stage. *Will* is the basic strength essential to this stage. For the black child a double whammy begins to emerge through the negative image of self which is picked up through the "looking glass" of a racist society.

The third stage begins roughly in the third year of life, the play age, where the child begins to think of himself in terms of what he imagines he can be. The challenge or crisis is between *initiative vs. guilt,* with *purpose* as the basic strength.

By school age, about 5, a child enters the stage where the challenge is *industry vs. inferiority,* where the issue is *competence* or personal mastery. The need is not merely for competence, but more fundamentally, a sense of competence. For the black male we arrive here at a crucial issue. The black male's sense of competence portrayed on the basketball court, the boxing ring or dance floor will somehow often evaporate in more alien or antagonistic social situations. This paradox has been alluded to by the poet, Haki Madhubuti. Toward the end of latency, as we begin the preparation of the year of THE PASSAGE, the challenge or crisis becomes *identity vs. identity confusion,* and *fidelity* in identity is an issue which will rage throughout adolescence as the child contends with the question "who am I"? THE PASSAGE is meant to help the boy begin to think of himself as a social man, however we as a people may define it.

At the same time as we focus upon the adolescent stage, where identity is king, we will have an eye on the later stages of young adulthood, middle and old age. The young adult must struggle with love and meet the crisis between *intimacy vs. isolation.* In the mature adulthood stage, generativity vs. stagnation, or making a contibution equal to one's potential, the basic strength is *care* Finally, in old age, *wisdom* becomes the basic strength in the crisis of *integrity vs. despair.* All these are important to the complete development of the black boy. [19]

However, it is at the point of *competence,* the sense of personal competence and mastery, leading into the problem of identity (racial and manhood identity) that we have arrived at THE PASSAGE. Yet if the child has not received an element of basic trust in the environment in the first year of life, he has started out on a ruptured or distorted linkage to a full and favorable identity with his people, his surroundings and, therefore, himself.

This strikes at the heart of the much despised, "black self-hatred", so much rejected by black intellectuals of late but existing continually by whatever name. And it is connected to the problems of *autonomy vs. shame* and *doubt, initiative vs. guilt,* as well as competence *(industry vs. inferiority)* and identity confusion.

Franz Fanon,[20] although not expressly pinpointing developmental stages, independently parallelled and expanded our insights into the impact of social oppression on psychobiological wellbeing. From these works, we arrive at the crucial age of departure and our endeavors here. Our understanding of the challenge that lies before us sets this stage concretely at the moment of transition from latency to adolesence.

We have set the age for completion of the Year of PASSAGE at 12. In addition to psychological and sociological principles, the age of 12 is supported by both sacred and secular tradition. Moreover the boy is poised to enter physical puberty where we are able to catch him prior to the point of no return.

We are able to intervene at the time many boys start down the treadmill to delinquency. It is at the threshold of engulfment by the peer group and peer pressures, self conscious and ambivalent, perhaps confused, noticeable physical changes and emerging passion. At the same time as he undergoes his physical metamorphosis, we usher him through a psychosocial transformation, including a cultural awakening.

As things now stand, no one tells the black boy concretely when he has become a man. Therefore, many grow up never fully realizing that they have become a man, though various legal sanctions open access to minor vices and privileges routinely at 18 or 21.

Lacking the initiation rites of our African ancestors, or even variations of those still popular among some other ethnic and religious groups, the black boy is left to his own devices. This is complicated by the fact that the most spectacular success of himself and his peers in boyhood is in the area of sports and entertainment and then repeats itself as the most glaring success ladder among adult black men. However, the boy who enjoys success on the basketball court may be on the way to riches and fame but it is seldom fulfilling throughout the life cycle.

THE PASSAGE will set in motion the machinery to divest the boy of childhood and develop full citizenship as a reponsible and productive man in the black community.

YEAR OF THE PASSAGE

A.   The year of the passage begins with the 11th birthday. However, considering the psychology of motivation and commitment, it is important to give the impression that the boy calls for the actual beginning of the experience. Once THE PASSAGE has been popularized and is universally accepted by black people, almost all boys will find it difficult to wait for the 11th birthday to begin their duties. Meanwhile it is up to the parents to ensure that the initiative is taken by the boy without excessive delay. It can be a delay of a week or even a month. But it is important that the boy not delay too long as he will miss the foundation of the first month's activities. He should be strongly expected to call for his PASSAGE on his 11th birthday.

B.   Once the boy takes the initiative, he has already taken the first step towards responsibility. This collaboration between the parent and the child is duplicated considerably by the children's conversion to a parent's religion. The same has been said of some boys who become priests.

C. THE PASSAGE activities should be flexible so as to allow each boy's creativity to flourish. The requirements offer a challenge and a commitment, a preparation for the responsibilities of adulthood. The paramount focus should be an orientation and exposure to the knowledge and resources that will assist the boy in wise, responsible decisions as he continues chronologically towards adulthood and thereafter.

D. Some activities are to be completed before the 12th birthday or the day of THE PASSAGE celebration:

1. The Log
2. An awareness and understanding of self.
3. An awareness and understanding of immediate and extended family.
4. Service to neighborhood and community.
5. Adopt a senior citizen.
6. Educational opportunities, including and beyond public schools, i.e. higher education.
7. Discipline and responsibility.
8. Preparation of *THE PASSAGE* CEREMONY.[21]

IMPLEMENTATION OF PRE-PASSAGE CEREMONY

A. THE LOG

Beginning with the moment the boy enters *THE PASSAGE* year, a record should be kept by the boy and periodically checked by the parent(s) or guardian and the PRESIDING ADULT. (See the Passage script for keys to identify the Presiding Adult). This may include pictures. clippings, notations, articles and other materials pertaining to his transition.

B. AN AWARENESS AND UNDERSTANDING OF SELF

The boy is made to understand that an awareness of self includes knowing your past. This is done through histroy, literature, music, cultural events, family testimony and lore.

1) For instance, he may be expected to read a certain number of books and to write reviews of them. These reviews are placed in the LOG. Select some black periodicals (magazines or newspapers) to be read each month throughout the year of *THE PASSAGE*.

One book should be about Africa, one black (American) history, and one in current or contempory economic, political and cultural issues. Parents and the Presiding Adult will monitor and review the boy's work on the projects.

2) With the advice and guidance of the parents and Presiding Adult, the boy should endeavor to gain an understanding and appreciation of beauty in the context of the black and African race.

C. AN UNDERSTANDING OF IMMEDIATE AND EX-TENDED FAMILY

A full list is made of relationships and whereabouts of each relative, beginning with immediate family. This project begins with immediate family and goes back as far as possible. Letters may be written to family members in this quest for knowledge of other relatives and ancestors.

D. SERVICE TO NEIGHBORHOOD AND COMMUNITY

The boy should talk with parents or teachers, spiritual leader or some other responsible persons about some service he can perform for his neighborhood or community.

E. ADOPT A SENIOR CITIZEN

"Adopt" a senior citizen to talk with and help from time to time, such as running errands or doing light chores on at least a once-a-month or weekly basis.

F. EDUCATIONAL OPPORTUNITIES INCLUDING AND BEYOND PUBLIC SCHOOLS, i.e. HIGHER EDUCATION

With the assistance and guidance of the parent and or PRESIDING Adult, inquiry and reflection should from time to time be made regarding possible future careers and educational preparation. The boy should inquire about special programs, schools, training and scholarships available. The boy should have or obtain a Public Library Card.

G. DISCIPLINE AND RESPONSIBILITY

This includes going about appropriate chores in a timely and self-generating or independent way. The boy should begin to practice conspicuous courtesy and appropriate obedience toward parents and elders as a model for life. The boy should begin to practice courtesy and respect for girls and women. The boy should practice respect, care and protectiveness toward younger children. The boy should contact or communicate with six elected officials or candidates (at least three black ones) on matters of concern to the boy or affecting his neighborhood. These issues should be discussed before and after with parents, teachers and other responsible adults.

H. PREPRATION FOR PASSAGE

Two days before THE PASSAGE ceremony, the boy is taken to the Presiding Adult or other responsible adult's home to complete preparation for THE PASSAGE ceremony. He spends the day and night before THE PASSAGE at the Presiding Adult's home.

While there, the boy

1)   will complete a spiritual fast

2)   practice and polish his speech

3)   is encouraged through appropriate questioning to participate in appropriate discussions with adults

4)   reviews and finalizes THE LOG

THE PASSAGE*

*For optimal use of *the celebration*, please read *"THE COM-MITMENT"* in the front of this manual before proceeding.

STYLE:

>Like churches, weddings, Barmitvahs, Kwanzaas, cotillions, fraternal organizations and prayer meetings, *THE PASSAGE* ceremony or celebration will vary from time to time, place to place and family to family according to group style and practice. however, the script presented here. though simplistic on the face of it, has been worked out according to concrete and important psychological principles as well as anthropological and sociological considerations. (see THE COMMITMENT for further details)

SETTING:

>Any facility such as a place where one would have a wedding, Kwanzaa, graduation or other milestone event.

PARTICIPANTS:

>The Boy (on 12th birthday or shortly thereafter)
>Parent or Parents
>Adults from extended family and neighborhood
>Grandparents (if available)
>Extended family includes:
>1) anybody related to the boy by blood
>2) anybody related to the boy in law
>3) play brothers, sisters, mothers, fathers, cousins

4) friends and mates of the relatives
5) any acceptable person with a supportive interest in the boy's development

USHERS:
Well disciplined teenage boys who, preferably, have gone through *PASSAGE.*

PRESIDING ADULT (ceremony leader):
this might include: pastors, or any other religious practitioners of your choice or/and persons who exhibit transcending wisdom, respect, responsibility and commitment)

SOLOIST AND INSTRUMENTALIST

TEACHERS AND COUNSELORS:
(These include recreational persons, coaches, and church school teachers, scout leaders, helpers and personages the boy can look up to)[21]

THE PASSAGE CELEBRATION

OPENING:

Guests are gathered and seated in the place of *PASSAGE.* The mood is one of joy and anticipation. Care must be taken not to be too loud or boisterous or to distract from the seriousness of the occasion. Once the ceremony begins, the audience must come to complete silence. This silence should be maintained with vigilance until the appropriate moments for expression.

PROCESSIONAL:

Music can be sacred or secular, with significant and appropriate inspirational content. Relatives enter from rear of the assembly. They include aunts, uncles, cousins, godparents, sisters and brothers, grandparents, mother and father. Some distance should be placed between entrance of grandparents and parents and other kin.

When parents are halfway to the Presiding Adult, the boy enters from front of assembly and joins his parents or guardian. Then all three will advance the remaining distance to join the designated spot for the ceremony. Other members of the processional are seated in reserved front row seats.

PRESIDING ADULT:

(Parents and boy are facing the Presiding Adult)

Presiding Adult explains the meaning of MANHOOD, its obligations, and responsibility to elders, men, women, children, race, community and nation.

(At the conclusion, the Presiding Adult faces the boy)

Presiding Adult:

"Whose manhood do we honor this day?"

THE BOY OR BOYS:

Give name or names (if more than one crossing into PASSAGE at single ceremony)

PRESIDING ADULT:

"Why do you wish to accept the passage to manhood?"

THE BOY:

"The time has come and I am ready to accept my responsibilities".

PRESIDING ADULT: (Facing audience)

"Do you approve of (name of boy) seeking responsibility for manhood?"

AUDIENCE:

Give expressions of praise and approval.

(At this point parents or guardians should be seated)

Adult)

PRESIDING ADULT:

Reads aloud and interprets an inspirational poem: e.g. "If We Must Die" by Claude McKay (available from local library — to be fetched by boy before the ceremony)

SOLOIST/AUDIENCE:

"Lift Every Voice and Sing" (the black anthem, also located and obtained in advance by the boy)

MEN OF THE AUDIENCE:

Read aloud: "I AM A BLACK MAN" (see appendix)

WOMEN OF THE AUDIENCE:

Respond with appropriate expression.

FRIEND OR RELATIVE:

A word of praise for the boy.

MOTHER:

Praise, advice and inspiration for her son.

FATHER OR MALE GUARDIAN

(or male person with long-standing supportive interest in the boy):
Words of encouragement and inspiration

THE BOY:

Stands, acknowledges leader, parents or guardian, relatives and friends.

Reads or recites his prepared speech. This speech should include: some mention of his growth both educationally and spiritually; some word of how his affiliations (clubs and organizations) have enhanced him; books that have left a deep impression; some mention of his community and people dear to him. A general sharing of feelings encountered up to now. If possible, mention of how he plans to contribute to his race and nation as a man.
(note: this speech is prepared with the guidance of the Presiding Adult)

AUDIENCE:

Acknowledges speech and parents. This includes a period of individual testimony in praise of the boy.

PRESIDING ADULT:

Turns to the boy and proclaims:
"(name of boy), we welcome you to the honored realm, challenges and responsibilities, of black manhood."

(Immediate cheers and approval from the audience. An atmosphere of joy and celebration should be maintained as the instrumentalist (drum, piano, organ, etc...) plays "Lift Every Voice and Sing.")

PRESIDING ADULT, THE BOY AND THE PARENT(S):

Proceed to the point of exit.

AUDIENCE:

Ushered out by the ushers to receive the boy with handshakes, congratulations and complimentary gestures.

THE FEAST

(African or traditional — with an abundance of fruits and vegetables)

(The music continues, along with the accolades, throughout the feast.)

FOOTNOTES & REFERENCES

1. William Raspberry, " Black Underclass," Washington Post Writers Group, syndicated column published in the *San Francisco Examiner*, June 22, 1985; p. C10.

2. M.A. Farber "Destiny and a Tragedy," and Marcia Chambers, "Attack on Officer Charged." subsidiary articles in "Brother of Slain Student Indicted: City Officer Cleared in the Killing." *The New York Times*. July 4, 1985, pp. 1, 12.

3. Richard Stengel and Jack E. White, "Immigrants - Blacks: Resentment Tinged with Envy, " *Time* July 9, 1985, pp. 56, 58.

4. Margaret Bush Wilson, KDIA Radio, San Francisco, California, circa 1975.

5. Nathan Hare and Julia Hare, *The Endangered Black Family*, San Francisco, Black Think Tank, pp. 130-132.

6. See special issues on "Black Psychology" in *Black Books Bulletin*, Chicago: The Institute of Positive Education, circa 1974-77. Also, Patricia Gurin, Gerald Gurin, Rosina C. Lao, and Muriel Beattie, "Internal-External Control of the Motivational Dynamics of Negro Youth," in Stanley S. Cuteman, ed., *Black Psyche: The Modal Personality Patterns of Black Americans*, Berkeley, California: The Glendessary Press, 1972, pp. 289-306.

7. See Arnold R. Pilling, "Matriarchy" in Julius Gould and William L. Kolb (ed.), *A Dictionary of the Social Sciences*, York: The Free Press of Glencoe, A Division of Macmillan, 1964, pp. 416. See also Steven Goldberg, "Anthropology and the Limits of Societal Variation," *The Inevitability of Patriarchy*, New York: William Morrow & Co., 1974, p. 36.

8. Fred Hapgood, *Why Males Exist*, New York: New American Library, 1979, *passim*.

9. Joseph Scott & James Stewart, "The Institutional Decimation of the Black Male," *The Western Journal of Black Studies*. Pullman, Washington: Washington State University Press, 1978. See also Jacquelyn Johnson Jackson, "But Where Are the Men?" *The Black Scholar*, Vol. 3, No. 4, December, 1971, pp. 30-41. (later adapted for *Ebony*).

Lawrence Gary, "The Black Male," *The Urban Research Review*, Institute of Urban Affairs, Howard University, 1980. Nathan Hare, "What Black Intellectuals Misunderstand about the Black Family," *Black World*, v. XXV, No. 5, May, 1976, pp. 20-33. Nathan and Julia Hare, "The Ressurection of the Black Male: The $1 Trillion Misunderstanding, "*Black Male/Female Relationships*, San Francisco, Black Think Tank, v. 2, #1, 1980, pp. 33-42.

10. Testimony of Sam Eubahkubokum, San Francisco State University class in Black Child Development, Spring semester, 1985. See also Lige Dailey, "Playing the Dozens: A Psycho-Historical Examination of an African American Ritual," Unpublished Ph.D. dissertation, Berkeley: The Wright Institute, May, 1985.

11. Wade Nobles, "Black Child Development, " *Perspectives*, (Official Newsletter of the San Francisco Bay Area Black

Psychologists), Spring, 1985. See also: Oba Tshaka, *The Legacy of Malcolm X,* Chicago: Third World Press, 1983. Francis Cress Welsing, lecture at the Pan-African Conference, Compton State College, Compton, California, March 15, 1985, Maulana Karenga, *Introduction to Black Studies.* Inglewood, California: Kawaida Publications, 1982. Robert Staples, *Black Masculinity,* Sausalito, California: Black Scholar Books, 1978.

12. Harry Morgan, "Neonatal Precocity and the Black Experience," *Negro Educational Review,* Vol. 27, 1976, pp. 129-134. See Also Janice Hale, "Physical Precocity and Movement," *Black Children: Their Roots, Culture and Learning Styles,* Provo, Utah: Brigham Young University Press, 1982, pp. 75-79.

13. Daryll Forde, Meyer Fortes, Victor W. Turner, Max Gluckman (ed.), *Les Rites de Passage: Essays on the Ritual of Social Relations,* Manchester, England: University of Manchester Press, 1966, p. 2. We are especially indebted to Jomo Kenyatta, *Facing Mt. Kenya: The Tribal Life of the Gikuyu,* New York: Vintage Books, 1965, for insight and sensitivity to the deeper cultural, psychological and sociological meanings of ritual and ceremony in personal and social development.

14. Forde *et. al.,* "Three Symbols of Passage in Ndembu Circumcision Ritual: An Interpretation," In Max Gluckman, ed., *op. cit.,* p. 34.

15. *Ibid.,* p. 37. See also Yehudi A. Cohen, "Ceremonies in the Second Stage of Puberty," *Childhood to Adolescence: Legal Systems and Incest Taboos,* Chicago: Aldine Publishing Co., 1964.

16. Cf. Konrad Lorenz, *On Aggression,* tr. by Marjorie Kerr Wilson, New York: Harcourt, Brace & World, 1966.

Authors' Files, Cf. from Children's Hospital Medical Centers Library Notation number A32, December 1977.

18. Erik H. Erikson, *Childhood and Society*, New York: W.W. Norton & Co., 1950, 1963, *passim*. See also Erik H. Erikson, *The Life Cycle Completed*, New York: W.W. Norton & Co., 1982, *passim*.

19. *Ibid.*, Chart 2, "Major Stages in Psychosocial Development," pp. 56, 57. See also Jimes Comer, M.D. and Alvin Poussaint, M.D., *Black Child Care*, New York: Pocket Books, 1975, p. 14.

20. Frantz Fanon, *Studies in a Dying Colonialism*, tr. by Haakon Chevalier, New York: Grove Press, 1968. Also, *The Wretched of the Earth*, tr. by Constance Farrington, New York, Grove Press, 1967, *passim*.

21. Frank T. Fair, *Orita for Black Youth: An Initiation into Christian Adulthood*, Valley Forge, Pa.: Judson Press, 1977. NOTE: on page 15, the old folks were paraphrasing or excerpting Langston Hughes' perennially popular poem, "Mother to Son." Cf. Jawanza Kunjufu, *Countering the Conspiracy to Destroy Black Boys, 1984*. Maulana Karenga, *Kawaida Theory*, 1980.

Appendix

I AM A BLACK MAN

by Nathan Hare

The evidence of anthropology now suggests that I, the black man, am the original man, the first man to walk this vast imponderable earth. I, the black man, am an African, the exotic quintessence of a universal blackness. I have lost by force my land, my language, in a sense my life, I will seize it back so help me.

Toward that end, if necessary, I will crush the corners of the earth, and this world will surely tremble, until I, the black man, the first and original man, can arm in arm with my woman, erect among the peoples of the universe a new society, humane to its cultural core, out of which at long last will emerge, as night moves into day, the first truly human being that the world has ever known.

BRING THE BLACK BOY TO MANHOOD

"I can only say hail Hare! Nathan and Julia Hare provided us with a clear ceremonial passage route for our Black boys to become socially responsible men. A men. One cannot be a "man" without a man-plan. Here then, is the hare-line to follow: a refined, outlived, well designed ceremonial "Year of the passage" that brings the African American boy to his manhood. And the beautiful part of this passage plan is the boy's total participation in his own actualization. Oh happy day!" --Dr. Gwendolyn Goldsby Grant, Advice Columnist, ESSENCE magazine

"Nathan and Julia Hare in this decade of confusion continue to offer clear, no-nonsense, disciplined direction for serious Black development. Their, *Endangered Black Family* is one of the most important analyses of Black life to appear in the last 15 years. Now, with the publication *Bringing the Black Boy to Manhood: The Passage,* they have created a self-help manual for young Black males that every black home should own. The Hares are not only impassioned observers of the Black World, but are scholar-activities that are setting new standards of scholarship and advocacy for Black Social Science." --Haki R. Madhubuti, Poet, Publisher, Editor Educator

"Congratulations on your work and on your timely service to our people." --Myrtle E. Gray, Pres, National Association of Colored Women's Clubs, Inc.

"The rites of passage to manhood is an absolute necessity for Black men in America." --Preston Wilcox, Pres AFRAM Library Files Harlem, NY

"**WHAT A GREAT IDEA. I've been saying this needs to be done for years.**" --William Merritt, Ph.D., Pres, National Association of Black Social Workers

"**... a unique and indispensable contribution ... right on time, in the nick of time ... a superior roadmap ...**" --Asa Hilliard, Ph.D., Distinguished Professor of Education, Georgia State University

"**... this work is long overdue ... Its strength lies not only in the clear, concise and well-developed arguments it presents, but also in the functional prescription and timely challenge it poses ...**" --Maulana Karenga, Ph.D., creator of Kwanzaa; The Institute of Pan-African Studies, Los Angeles

"**Finally, the (black) follow-up to Jomo Kenyatta's world African rites of passage into manhood.**" --Jawanza Kunjufu, author, *Conspiracy to Destroy Black Boys.*

"**... an excellent idea ... It has worked in other cultures for thousands of years. Why not ours?**" --Henry Lucas, D.D.S., Member, Martin Luther King Commission, Calfiornia

"**... a needed and creative approach ... can become a meaningful to black people as Kwanzaa.**" --Oba Tshaka, The National Black United Front; Chair, Black Studies, San Francisco State University

ABOUT THE AUTHORS

Dr. Nathan Hare holds two Ph.D.'s (in clinical psychology and sociology). Dr. Hare was a prominent pioneer of the "black studies" movement of the late 1960's at Howard University and San Francisco State University, where he was the first person hired to coordinate a black studies program in the United States. Dr. Hare, a recent winner of the National Award for distinguished scholarly contributions to black studies, from the National Council for Black Studies, is in the private practice of psychotherapy in San Francisco.

Julia Hare has won the Outstanding Educator Award for the city of Washington, D.C., from the Junior Chamber of Commerce and the World Book Encyclopedia. During an extensive career with ABC and the Golden West Broadcasters, she won the Abraham Lincoln Award for radio broadcasting. With her husband , she is co-author of the highly acclaimed book, *The Endangered Black Family* and *How To Find and Keep A (BMW) Black Man Working.* Dr. Hare has appeared on CNN and Company, Politically Incorrect, Geraldo, Sally Jesse Raphael among others.